What's the Issue?

WHAT'S GUN CONTROL?

By Kate Rogers

Published in 2018 by
KidHaven Publishing, an Imprint of Greenhaven Publishing, LLC
353 3rd Avenue
Suite 255
New York, NY 10010

Designer: Seth Hughes
Editor: Katie Kawa

Photo credits: Cover (top) NEstudio/Shutterstock.com; cover (bottom) RubberBall Productions/ Brand X Pictures/Getty Images; p. 4 giftlegacy/iStock/Thinkstock; p. 5 (top) Spencer Platt/Getty Images; p. 5 (bottom) Daniel Acker/Bloomberg via Getty Images; p. 6 Bettmann/Contributor/ Getty Images; p. 7 Ryan Rodrick Beiler/Shutterstock.com; p. 8 courtesy of ATF via Getty Images; p. 9 (top) JanSommer/Shutterstock.com; p. 9 (bottom) Vakrish/Shutterstock.com; p. 10 Bill Clark/CQ Roll Call/Getty Images; p. 11 Drew Angerer/Getty Images; p. 12 Andrey_Popov/ Shutterstock.com; p. 13 digicomphoto/iStock/Thinkstock; p. 14 JIM WATSON/AFP/Getty Images; p. 15 sframephoto/iStock/Thinkstock; p. 16 Smart/iStock/Thinkstock; p. 17 Michael Loccisano/ Getty Images; p. 18 digitalreflections/Shutterstock.com; p. 20 Tatomm/iStock/Thinkstock; p. 21 splendens/iStock/Thinkstock.

Cataloging-in-Publication Data

Names: Rogers, Kate.
Title: What's gun control? / Kate Rogers.
Description: New York : KidHaven Publishing, 2018. | Series: What's the issue? | Includes glossary and index.
Identifiers: ISBN 9781534525092 (pbk.) | 9781534524415 (library bound) | ISBN 9781534525108 (6 pack) | ISBN 9781534524422 (ebook)
Subjects: LCSH: United States. Constitution. 2nd Amendment–Juvenile literature. | Firearms–Law and legislation–United States–History–Juvenile literature. | Gun control–United States–History– Juvenile literature. | Firearms ownership–Juvenile literature. | Firearms owners–Legal status laws, etc.–United States–Juvenile literature.
Classification: LCC KF3941.A435 2018 | DDC 323.4'3–dc23

Printed in the United States of America

CPSIA compliance information: Batch #CW18KL: For further information contact Greenhaven Publishing LLC, New York, New York at 1-844-317-7404.

Please visit our website, www.greenhavenpublishing.com. For a free color catalog of all our high-quality books, call toll free 1-844-317-7404 or fax 1-844-317-7405.

CONTENTS

Strong Feelings About Guns

Many Americans own guns. The right to own a gun has been part of American life for hundreds of years. It's in the Bill of Rights, which spells out the rights granted to all U.S. citizens.

Most gun owners never use a gun to hurt people, but some people do use guns to hurt others. Because of this, U.S. citizens and leaders often call for better methods of regulating, or governing, the sale and use of guns. This is known as gun control. Many people strongly support gun control, but others strongly oppose it.

Facing the Facts 🔍

In a 2017 study, 30 percent of American adults said they owned a gun.

Gun control is an issue that brings up strong feelings in many Americans. Understanding both sides of the gun control **debate** is important.

The Second Amendment

Early Americans believed having the right to own and use guns was needed to form a strong militia, which is a group of citizens who can serve as a military force if necessary. This is why it was included in the Bill of Rights, which is the first 10 amendments, or changes, to the U.S. **Constitution**.

The right to "keep and bear Arms," or **weapons** such as guns, is **protected** under the Second Amendment to the U.S. Constitution. When people fight against gun control, they often use the Second Amendment to back up their argument.

Facing the Facts 🔍

During the American Revolution, battles against the British were fought by militias. The Second Amendment was created out of fear that militias would be needed again to fight a central government that was too powerful.

The Second Amendment has been at
the center of many debates throughout
American history. People often argue
about how it can be applied to weapons
far deadlier than any the Founding Fathers

New Guns, New Laws

The first guns used in what became the United States were most likely brought to the New World by the Spanish hundreds of years before the Second Amendment was written. As times changed and guns became more **dangerous**, it became clear that new laws were needed to protect Americans.

In 1934, the National Firearms Act (NFA) was passed. It put a tax on and required **registration** for certain guns, such as shotguns, rifles, and machine guns. More than 50 years later, the Firearms Owners' Protection Act was passed to ban the ownership of machine guns made after 1986.

Facing the Facts 🔍

The Bureau of Alcohol, Tobacco, Firearms and Explosives (ATF) is the part of the U.S. government that deals with the illegal use of guns.

early American gun

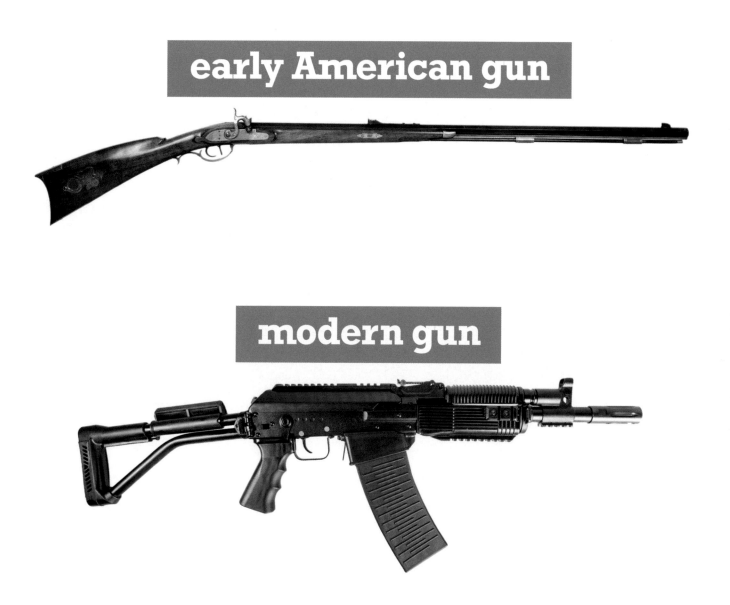

modern gun

The guns made today are very different from the guns made when the Second Amendment was written. New laws have been needed to deal with these new, more powerful weapons.

Stopping Mass Shootings

Over time, guns have become deadlier, which has led to an increase in mass shootings in the United States. The exact meaning of "mass shooting" is different depending on the person or group talking about it. In most cases, it means an act of gun **violence** in which at least four people are shot.

After a mass shooting occurs, people often talk about making gun control laws stronger. They want to do whatever they can to keep these events from happening, and they believe gun control is the best way to do that.

Facing the Facts

A 2017 study showed that 44 percent of Americans said they know someone who has been shot.

VEGAS STRONG

On October 1, 2017, more than 50 people died and more than 500 people were injured in a mass shooting in Las Vegas, Nevada. It was the deadliest mass shooting in U.S. history to date. After it, many people called for stronger gun control laws to make the country safer.

Universal Background Checks

One of the gun control measures people often call for is a better system of **background** checks for people who want to buy guns. In 1993, the Brady Handgun Violence Protection Act led to the creation of the National Instant Criminal Background Check System (NICS). It's still used today to keep dangerous people from buying guns.

Licensed gun dealers must perform background checks before selling someone a gun. However, unlicensed sellers, such as people online, don't have to do this. A universal background check system would end this practice and require all gun sellers to run background checks.

Request for
Criminal Background Check

By signing and submitting Criminal Background Check, I certify that this application is complete a all information provided is true and accurate and contains no willful falsifications misrepresentation. I understand that falsifications, representations, or omissions may disqualif from consideration to this position. I hereby authorize responsible person to contact curre previous employers for verification, conduct a background investigation, and check my

12

Full legal
Last Name

Name Phone

Facing the Facts 🔍

As of 2016, around 90 percent of Americans said they supported universal background checks for gun buyers.

The NICS is used by licensed gun sellers to find out if someone isn't allowed to own a gun for legal reasons, such as being guilty of a violent crime.

Banning Assault Weapons

When guns were first used, they took a long time to load and could only fire one shot at a time. Today, that's no longer the case. A kind of gun called a semiautomatic assault weapon can load itself between shots so people don't have to stop shooting to reload their gun.

Assault weapons can be used to kill many people very quickly. Because of this, a law was passed in 1994 to ban them. However, that law **expired** in 2004 and wasn't **renewed.** Now it's up to each state to decide whether or not to ban these guns.

Facing the Facts

As of 2017, seven states and the District of Columbia have laws banning assault weapons.

In June 2016, the U.S. Supreme Court ruled that state bans on assault weapons didn't go against the Second Amendment.

Gun Control Around the World

Gun control laws in the United States are very different from gun control laws in many other countries around the world. For example, universal background checks are common in many countries. In the United Kingdom, the only people who are allowed to legally own a gun are those who've shown that they need a gun for work, hunting, or collecting.

Australia is often used as an example of a country with successful gun control laws. After a mass shooting in 1996, new gun laws banned many weapons. As of 2017, there have been no more mass shootings in Australia.

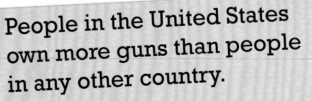

Facing the Facts

People in the United States own more guns than people in any other country.

Gun buyback **programs** worked in Australia and are used in many U.S. cities to get guns off the streets. These programs give people money for turning in guns.

Guns and Freedom

Some Americans argue that just because other countries around the world have strong gun control laws, that doesn't mean the United States has to follow them. Gun ownership and freedom have been tied together in the United States since its earliest days. Today, Americans sometimes state that gun control laws are unconstitutional.

One group that fights for the rights of U.S. gun owners is the National Rifle Association (NRA). It was created in 1871, and today, it's known for educating people about guns, as well as working to protect Second Amendment rights.

Facing the Facts 🔍

As of 2017, one in five U.S. gun owners stated that they belonged to the NRA.

Main Reasons Americans Own a Gun

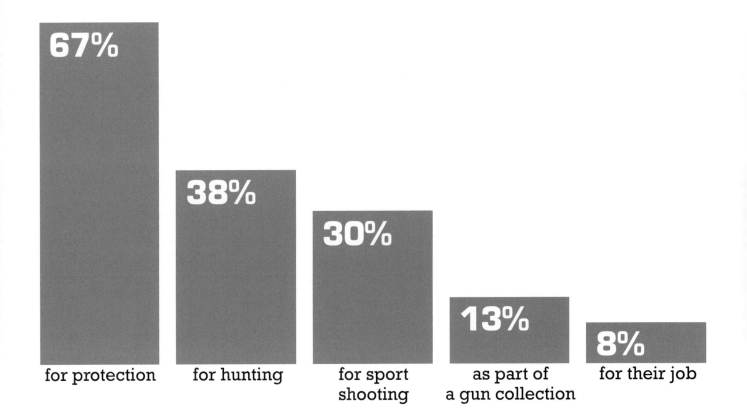

67% for protection

38% for hunting

30% for sport shooting

13% as part of a gun collection

8% for their job

This graph is from the Pew Research Center, which reports on Americans' opinions of different issues. It shows what percent of U.S. gun owners have guns for certain reasons. Groups such as the NRA believe these are all good reasons that should be protected.

A Country Divided

Gun control is an issue that **divides** Americans. On one side are people who believe safety is worth giving up some freedoms. On the other side are people who believe guns in the right people's hands make America safer. They believe the right to own a gun is an important part of life in America, and they want to protect that right.

The debate over freedom and safety has been going on for many years in the United States. It's something all Americans need to learn about to help build a country where rights are protected but citizens feel safe.

Facing the Facts   🔍

Almost 75 percent of U.S. gun owners believe gun ownership is an important part of feeling free.

WHAT CAN YOU DO?

Write to your leaders about gun control laws.

Listen to people with different opinions on gun control to understand their point of view.

Learn more facts about gun control.

Raise money for people who have been harmed by guns.

If you feel strongly about gun control, these are some of the things you can do to keep learning about this issue and the people on both sides of the gun control debate.

GLOSSARY

background: The total of a person's life experience and education.

constitution: The basic laws by which a country, state, or group is governed.

dangerous: Not safe.

debate: An argument or discussion about an issue, generally between two sides.

divide: To separate into different groups.

expire: To come to an end.

licensed: Given official permission to do something.

program: A plan under which action may be taken toward a goal.

protect: To keep safe.

registration: The act of entering on an official list.

renew: To continue something for a new period of time.

violence: The use of force to harm someone.

weapon: Something used to cause harm.

FOR MORE INFORMATION

WEBSITES

The Bill of Rights: A Transcription

www.archives.gov/founding-docs/bill-of-rights-transcript

The National Archives presents visitors with the full text of the Bill of Rights, including the Second Amendment.

Gun Safety

kidshealth.org/en/kids/gun-safety.html

No matter how people feel about gun control, most support teaching children proper safety measures around guns, and this KidsHealth website explains gun safety in a way that is easy to understand.

BOOKS

Kevin, Brian. *Gun Rights & Responsibilities*. Minneapolis, MN: ABDO Publishing, 2012.

Larson, Kristen W. *The Second Amendment: The Right to Bear Arms*. North Mankato, MN: Capstone Press, 2018.

Wittmann, Kelly. *The Right to Bear Arms*. New York, NY: Gareth Stevens Publishing, 2017.

INDEX